Student Street Style

Julia Kress

Booky-Books No. 2
RIT Press
Rochester, New York

Copyright © 2025 Rochester Institute of Technology and Julia Kress
No part of this book may be reproduced in any form or by any mechanical or electronic means without permission of the publisher and/or the copyright holders, except in the case of brief quotations.

Published and distributed by:
RIT Press
90 Lomb Memorial Drive
Rochester, New York 14623
https://press.rit.edu

Printed in the United States of America

ISBN 978-1-956313-30-7 (print)

We gather on the traditional territory of the Onöndowa'ga:' or "the people of the Great Hill."
In English, they are known as Seneca people, "the keeper of the western door." They are one of the six nations that make up the sovereign Haudenosaunee Confederacy.
We honor the land on which RIT was built and recognize the unique relationship that the Indigenous stewards have with this land. That relationship is the core of their traditions, cultures, and histories. We recognize the history of genocide, colonization, and assimilation of Indigenous people that took place on this land. Mindful of these histories, we work towards understanding, acknowledging, and ultimately reconciliation.

Designed by Marnie Soom | Background images from Adobe Stock

Personally, I tend to dress very practically. I like to be comfortable and don't want my outfit getting in the way of anything, so I usually end up just wearing pants and a t-shirt. Even so, this outfit can express a lot about myself. Walking around RIT's campus, it can be very inspiring to see the outfits students wear. There's such a wide variety of different styles people have, and it's really interesting to see what inspired them, as well as the deeper stories behind specific pieces of clothing and what they mean to the wearer. That's why I wanted to write this book: to get a chance to explore the stories behind people's outfits that you wouldn't get from just looking at them, as well as to share RIT's creativity and culture with a wider audience. My process for interviewing people was simple: I hung out in public places with a large volume of students such as the Quarter Mile and the SAU. I then approached anyone with an interesting outfit and asked them questions about it. All the photos in this book were taken by me, including the picture of me, which I got by balancing my phone on a makeshift stand consisting of cereal boxes, a paper-towel holder, and a chair.

"I really like the Y2K style. Even if I dress basic, I wanna dress basic like how they dressed back then. I feel like it's just so effortless. The fit right now is just, like, pink camo basically, but I like to switch it up a lot of the time. When I dress feminine, I like going all the way and just super going for it. I kinda just try shit. Like today it's rainy, and there's not a lot of people wearing super-bright colors, but I always like to be the one who is."

—Helena Winchester

"Usually I would say my favorite part of my outfit is the sweater, but today I think it's the green. I've never worn it under this sweater; I usually just wear white underneath it. So it's like, a little pop of color. I think I'm still kind of figuring out my style, but I like jewelry. I wanna get more into incorporating layering with necklaces, and mixing metals, like gold and silver. I didn't wear any rings today because I knew I was just gonna take them off. I usually don't even wear bracelets because I can't, like, write with them on. I usually go for earrings; that's my staple."

—Kimberly Tana

"I think I like to be loud. I need to be able to be spotted from across a courtyard, and I like jingly, flashy jewelry. If there's not sparkles, I'm doing something wrong. I notoriously do not have one style; my closet really ranges. I will wildly swing from one thing to another, but I think that's what's fun about it: you keep people on their toes. Some days I look like a My Little Pony threw up on me, and other days I look like I walked out of a Hot Topic. Sometimes my outfits are based on what I'm into that week. If I'm into a certain show or movie or book, I will very frequently try to base my outfits around characters that I'm really into at that point in time. Today I've been really stuck on 'Lying is the Most Fun a Girl Can Have Without Taking Her Clothes Off,' the old Panic! at the Disco song. So that has a harlequin vibe, and I was thinking, 'you know, I need to get into that sort of vibe today,' so that's what I'm going for."

—Kaelyn "Gil" Beeman

"I really like the fusion of hippie-goth; it's what I try to go for. 'Cause I'm super lazy, so it's a lot easier than doing full goth, and it's a lot softer too. I have vastly different styles, so usually I'll just wake up and feel it out. I like hippie-goth a lot, but some days when I'm just not feeling it, I'll go for more masculine streetwear. So it's like I have a spectrum of masc streetwear to feminine hippie-goth. Today actually I'm kind of in mourning, so I was originally getting dressed in a much more goth outfit today, and then I got a text letting me know, like, 'hey, a family friend passed away.' So I kind of toned down my outfit to be in that mourning head-space. I'm going to the funeral this weekend."

—April Caplette

"Personally I don't spend a lot of time thinking when I get dressed. I just pick a shirt and pants I wanna wear and then sleep with it. I like to wear just mundane clothes, sometimes street-wear, like t-shirts and baggy pants. I just think it's comfortable."

— Mika Seabo

"First of all, please ignore the fact that I'm covered in sawdust. I don't know why, but my favorite color probably changes every year. The last solid year and a half has been this pink, like my water bottle, for whatever reason. Back in high school, my sophomore/junior year, my favorite color was lavender, and I bought, like, fifteen different lavender sweaters. And I mean, I still like them, but now I have fifteen different pink sweaters to go with my fifteen different lavender sweaters. I really like this shirt I'm wearing; I have four different Strawberry Shortcake shirts. They're all from, like, the original Strawberry Shortcake era. And I think it's gotten pretty popular recently, as some sort of trend, but I'm all for it, man. I loved Strawberry Shortcake growing up. I had a McDonald's toy of Lemon Meringue that smelled like lemons, and that's why she was my favorite. I still have it in my closet somewhere."

—McKenna Barker

Acknowledgments

I'd like to thank my roommates, without whom this book would not be possible. Thanks for coming along with me to interview people for this book; I really appreciated the support.

About the Author

Julia Kress is a second-year industrial design student in RIT's School of Design. She eventually hopes to work in architecture, designing efficient and eco-friendly public spaces. Her dream job is to design unique playgrounds and public art installations. She was raised in upstate New York; if you were to take a map and draw a straight line from Rochester to the far east side of New York, that's where she's from. In her free time, she enjoys fiber arts such as knitting and quilting, even though they can be pretty time-consuming. She's been knitting the same scarf for over two years now and still hasn't finished it! She also likes to ski, and during Rochester's long winters, she races on RIT's alpine ski team. She has a dog named Anders whom she loves very much.